NAVIGATE YOURSELF

KETAKI SANE

INDIA · SINGAPORE · MALAYSIA

ISBN
Paperback 979-8-89673-766-7
Hardcase 979-8-89699-538-8

In loving memory of Sumedh.

This would have been yet another
wannabe self-help book,
had it not been for that incident.

And I would happily trade off the
very existence of this book,
to stop or at least delay
that incident from happening.

Throughout the book, all I am going to do is be selfish.

Seriously, right now I don't care about helping anyone. Because I have realised that, if everyone just helps just one person in their entire life, just one person, the entire planet will be better.

And that one person is you, yourself. And no one, not even the Divine can help you, if you constantly choose to be your own enemy.

By writing this, I am helping myself. I am documenting myself.

Without sounding rude, if you can do that to yourself by the end of his book, you will do yourself a huge favour.

The book had a different name before that *incident*. And somehow, this new name made more sense to me. Because that is what we all need right now, that is what we always needed as humans and that is what we will continue to need irrespective of the *yug* that we are born in.

And that is to *navigate yourself* and live your authentic self.

People everywhere (especially healers, psychics, modern age astrologers, tarot readers, aura readers and every such modality) are talking about the 5D plane today.

That the Earth is opening up to the 5D plane and spiritual growth as a concept is gaining more and more weightage and reality.

That also leaves us all susceptible to a whole bunch of wannabe healers (with all due respect to the authentic ones) to play with our minds. Earlier it was religion and now it's like spirituality ki *dukaan* in every *galli.*

Every now and then one video pops up with a man or a woman saying "do you know why the law of attraction doesn't work for you?", "do you know why you are not able to manifest?"

And like a little hopeful dreamy eyed puppy, we enter the enticing world of 'hoping to make our dreams a reality' trying to manifest, learning different ways to do it right.

The primary reason I am penning this down (and all genuine healers will agree) is to ask you to take your power back from all those you are following out of desperation.

Answer a simple question, YOU have been living with yourself for the past xyz years, right?

Then do you think some third person knows you better or you know yourself better?

What makes you think some random person can help you better than you can help yourself? By random person, I mean all the external triggers that keep influencing us, robbing us of the time and opportunities to connect with our own self.

The logical answer is YOU know yourself better, you can help yourself better. It's like a map, you know your home-address like the back of your hand, YOU know where your home is, not other people.

Complications take over when you stop giving yourself the chance, the permission, the opportunity and the environment to 'know yourself' – again going by the map analogy, on the way home you find so many distractions and pseudo destinations, that you are bound to get lost and confused to the extent that you think where you have arrived is home, but you are probably far too away from your own authentic home.

And then you keep getting frustrated that you are not manifesting and fall prey to those videos of the law of attraction not working for you.

Those guys are not wrong. Their diagnosis of your condition is right. They have rightly tapped into the 'effect' that something that is so universal is not working for you. But they either are unable to or don't want to tap into the 'cause'.

It's like the classic pharmaceutical industry, that majorly makes money on symptom control, because who has the time and patience to sit and understand the cause.

What if you actually do that and realise you don't need those pills after all. What if you actually do that and realize you are not really sick, it is just a minor frequency misalignment. You would still feel lost. You will still feel lost and doubt yourself and question yourself, despite making the world's most significant discovery.

Why? Because you will see people around who are different from you and you want to feel belonged. You don't want to feel left out. So you tag along, become one with them.

That's how you get lost from reaching home. You have the map, you have the resources but you are too scared to just sit down with yourself and reflect; "Is this the direction for me?"; "Is this where my home is?"

If you still don't realise the gravity of the situation, let me make it simpler. Here comes one more analogy.

Let's say you are a certain kind of fruit, an apple. In the world of fruits, mango is the king of fruits, and everyone wants to be one.

As an apple, you are telling yourself and manifesting to become a mango. Will it ever work? No.

It is as simple as that. Instead, manifest to be a 'better apple'. Now is that possible? Yes.

But the problem is you don't identify yourself as an apple, you don't know who you are at the core.

And just because society glorifies mangoes, kiwis, avocados, you want to be that too. Just because society glorifies titles, hefty pay packs, luxury cars, you want that too without giving it a second's thought that it is probably not what your authentic self needs.

An apple has its own place in a bowl of fruit salad, right? And a tomato, although classified as a fruit, will never feel at home in a fruit salad.

The point is, you will be more valuable as who you are. If you try to desperately fit somewhere just because everyone is doing it, you will not only lose your own value but you will also spoil the dish at large.

There are a few instructions I have for you before you dive deeper.

1. Read random pages of Part 1: A to Z Navigator Tool. Pick random times of the day, with different states of mind, mostly when you are looking for an answer.
2. Read Part 2: FYS, preferably after finishing part 1, if it is your first time.
3. Once you have done reading and reflecting once, feel free to re-read and re-reflect with random pages, there's a possibility some reflections may differ considering how far you have navigated yourself and evolved as a person.
4. I have always found answers by randomly opening pages of certain books and I want all those books to bless this book to do the same for you.
5. My singulair objective in writing this is to make you independent, to show you how powerful you can be when you take back power from all those things & people who drain you, who delay you from meeting you, knowingly or unknowingly.
6. At the end of the book and even in between, there are a lot of blank pages; use them to document YOU. Write down the question you had before you opened a certain page,

write down your interpretation of what you read, write down how it helped you.

7. You never know, someday it could turn into a powerful book too. But don't do this with the objective of it turning into a book, do it because it is a favour to yourself.
8. Remember, what you are holding in your hands right now is a hybrid between a book and a journal, it is like a journook :) so ya don't share the same copy with others, it's your own personal journey of navigating yourself, finding your essence, your superpower.
9. Be selfish, by not giving this same copy to others, and gifting them a fresh copy because you want your loved ones to transform too, and your life will be better if they evolve and transform with you, so ya selfishness to the core, just done better, win win for all.
10. Remember to DM me and/or tag the Instagram Handle @themerakiwoman, after you reach home :) after you have tuned in to your home frequency.
11. Make a fresh list of manifestations from your home frequency, I assure you, it won't feel like a chase, it will feel very natural, very peaceful.
12. Bring your own innovation, imagination to play – use pencils, color pens, highlighters – make this journey as interesting as you can.

Chalo, see you on the other side, which in fact is your authentic side.

Happy Navigating Yourself.

You attract what you vibrate. And if you can vibrate at your own natural authentic self, you will attract what is meant for you. What is meant for you is what you need as a soul dressed in this human body.

Close your eyes for a minute. Visualize your loved ones. Recall some of your best memories with them, imagine some of the future memories you will make with them. Stay there, embrace it for a while. Now imagine someone very close, just gone, dead.

This will put a lot of things in perspective. I don't care if I am sounding rude or mean, I would rather be that, so that you wake up to the reality before actually losing someone close, before an *incident* happens and there is nothing you can trade off to make that void go away.

Life is not about chasing someone else's dreams, it is about attracting your own reality. I hope no one has to pay an irreversible price for realising that.

All our lives, people have always told us, *"yeh karo,woh karo"*, *"yeh karna chahiye, woh karna chahiye"* but somehow they always miss out on telling us, 'HOW to do' or 'HOW not to do it.'

So, these A,B,C's will act as small tools to help you navigate yourself and arrive at your authentic self.

Make your own list of A,B,C's by the end of this book and share it with me; would love to learn from you.

Contents

A

Ask Always, Assume Never

Do you know why a child always gets its tantrums met?

Because the child asks for it. In his/her own way – lovingly, stubbornly, crying – whatever it takes. And we as adults abide by their innocent rebels.

Don't you think, we as kids of the Divine should know that we need to ask, too.

Ask what. Ask how. Is the important thing here.

By 'what' I don't always mean, ask for material things – I want good grades, I want that promotion, etc. The Divine will give you that, it's not a worry but this is like a coupon deal, lasts only till it exists. If you want something like a lifetime subscription, you really need to learn to ask the right questions and the answers right for you will fall into your lap.

Questions like; what am I doing wrong, what is this pattern trying to teach me, what can I do right in this situation.

Asking right questions also helps you navigate life as an adult in a work environment and even in relationships.

A lot of what we will chat about here will keep circling back to your work, because as an adult, there are only two most life-impacting things we spend most of our time and energy on. Finding work that makes us happy and finding a partner that makes us happy. This book will talk more about work because love is a conversation for another book.

You know, asking the right questions came to me as a survival mode; survive in a corporate setting.

I got my first ever paycheck from my first ever internship at IMS ORG, today known as IQVIA or IMS Health, world's leading provider of information solutions to the pharmaceutical and healthcare industries.

The first few days I was so lost in a pool of sophisticated people who walked around like they had their shit together. I remember sort of getting cornered and teased as the new intern.

I was assigned to a person two to three years senior to me and she had started giving me a bad time for no reason within a week of my joining.

A batchmate of mine had also got placed there along with me and he seemed to have it together and that made me even more anxious because their was only one vacancy for PPO (pre-placement offer) and those of you who know anything about healthcare or market research in general would know that IQVIA is a very prestigious place to work.

Well so, after around 2 weeks of being there, trying to find my place, I had a sense of people calling us names – the lost intern & the smart intern.

And that's when it happened. A meeting was called upon by the head, that involved 6 people – 2 interns, 3 seniors and the project head. I guess at a juncture during a presentation the project head pointed directly at me and I am assuming looking at my frown lines asked me, "Is there any confusion, you, the intern?"

My throat literally went dry and I also saw those seniors sort of mocking me passively. Imagine this, a huge 1000 sq feet of a conference room, AC in full mode, 5 pairs of eyes looking at me – felt to me like the survival of that major project depended entirely on my confused shoulders.

I gulped and said in a timid voice, "I am unsure if I understood this inference, what if we read the data in so-n-so manner, I mean I could be wrong…"

That put the entire room on such a spot; as if that one confused intern was questioning the methodology of the analysis.

"Ya, let's try it that way." said the project head to the presenter.

The inference changed drastically and so did the energy in the room.

From that point on I held on to the art of asking questions (not to disrupt the energy of the room, not to question someone's knowledge, not to make myself feel superior), just generally asking open ended questions with the objective of finding better solutions.

So please, ask Life the right questions. Don't ask and run away before Life has a chance to answer it for you. Balance the asking with receiving.

Activity: Do you recall finding yourself in a similar situation? Did it go North or South for you? Did the questions lead to answers or it led to more questions?

Activity: Remember the time when you were a kid full of questions. Most of the time people around would be willing to answer them for you. Likewise with Life, it answers to those who ask it right and who are willing to listen.

Few Pro-tips on how to Ask right.

- **Curiosity over Judgement:**

Can you help me understand why this decision was made?" instead of *"Why did you do it this way?"*

- **Open ended over Yes-No**

"How do you see this project unfolding?" instead of "Do you see the project unfolding as per timelines?"

- **Intent over Interrogation**

"What are the pros and cons of this approach?" instead of "Don't you think this approach is wrong?"

- **Singles over Doubles**

Instead of "Why wasn't the project finished, and what can we do to fix it?" try "What challenges delayed the project?" followed by "What solutions can we explore?"

- **Verify over Conclude**

"If I understand correctly, you're suggesting... Is that right?"

- **Problem over Person**

Replace *"Why didn't you finish the task?"* with *"What challenges came up that delayed the task?"*

- **Stay open to the answers**

Frame your own set of signature-questions that get you answers.

My signature question: Will you help me help you…

B

Be a Bitch, Not a Bichari

Just doing a word play here. By bitch, what I really mean is, be a badass. Do not harm, take no shit. That is the mindset one needs to develop.

I want to put on a gender lens here before we *un-gender* it.

I read this quote that all women fall under either of these 2 categories – victim or villain.

When you see your mom sacrificing her needs for the family she is the *'aww, bichari'* person who is liked and appreciated. The day she starts putting her foot down, making time for herself, taking a stand for what she cares about, she is suddenly the *'aye haye selfish'* person.

If your dad helps your mom around in the kitchen, he is the 'aye haye kitna supportive husband'. Luckily for me, I grew up with parents sharing gender-roles and responsibility, they both stepped into each other's shoes from time to time, be it with earning the bread, be it making the bread.

But I speak for the vast majority, because I rarely saw that with my friends back in school or college and with my colleagues at work.

No one identifies a woman as the 'hero' who is taking charge of her own story. She is always made to choose and sacrifice, not encouraged to prioritize and delegate.

Biologically there is a certain bias towards women, in how opportunities come their way. Indra Nooyi, Former CEO Pepsico, spoke about how a woman's biological clock and her career graph are often competing with each other and how sixty-seventy percent mid-management women drop out every year.

If you are a woman reading this, I have 2 questions for you:

1. Are you getting into such a competitive corporate role because you are living someone else's dream?

What I mean by this is a lot of young girls grow up with the belief that boys are better than them or carry that hurt of a lame comment from a relative or parents *'kaash yeh ladka hoti'* and all they want to do is prove themselves.

So I repeat, are you chasing a dream because of this hurt or does working on that project actually brings you joy. There's no right or wrong to it, it's just a self-reflective question.

2. Are you getting into motherhood, an even more challenging role, because you are supposed to, because of some set society template?

I am of the very strong opinion that motherhood should be a choice, a woman should opt for it only when she is physically, financially, mentally, emotionally and spiritually ready. Even if the biological clock is ticking, it is all about 'yes now it feels right' or 'no now is still not the time.'

What is that, that you want and is there a way you can have it all, if that is what you want.

If you want to balance a career and a baby, go for it. Do you want to work for a decade, take a sabbatical and be a full time mom forever or for a while, go for it. Do you love being a full time mom and have the necessary financial support, go for it. Do you want to never be a mom, or are you unsure if you ever want to be, or want to take time to figure it out, go for it.

Do whatever you do, because it feels right for you. Not because someone else thinks it is right for you.

We become what we vibrate to. If you have been living the 'victim' narrative all your life, that is who will be. If you start living the 'hero' narrative, from this very point, you will attract better and more collaborative things for yourself.

Being a bitch only means, identify what you want and fight for it like a badass.

Do no harm, take no shit. Because if you take shit, you send a signal to the universe that you 'like shit' and the universe is very unbiased that way. You ask for shit in your actions and intention, that is what you will get.

My very heartfelt apologies to 'karma' which always gets called as 'bitch' – karma won't bite at you unless you have done something nasty. Karma is a peace-loving, tit for tat entity.

Now let's *un-gender* the next part of the conversation.

Have you ever played the victim card, knowingly or unknowingly? As a guy or a girl. I mean, life may have put you in a situation where you were once a victim (poor finances, fighting parents, break-ups, etc.) but things are better now, but you sort of keep doing the blame-game narrative in your head – so and so had happened, hence I can't do so and so.

I know your first instinct would be "Noooo, I will never self-victimize…" but keep asking yourself this, you may not be doing it on purpose, but it could have become a pattern that has grown over you.

Let me give you an example.

Go back to being a child learning to ride a bicycle. As a first time learner, you are open and curious about it. You are just getting a hold of it and you bump against something.

You either get up and teach yourself to be more careful, continue the ride. Or you teach yourself to stay away from it because you got hurt or because your friends laughed at you. Either of these now becomes your pattern, that you may apply to other areas of life too.

Someone very close to me made me realise that some of my patterns were holding me back. In ways I was being lenient on myself because something bad happened to me, I kept giving excuses and playing a victim card unknowingly. I was justifying my lack of effort because I was holding on to the bad thing instead of learning from it and going forward in life.

You are setting yourself up for failure, the moment you start taking comfort in being a victim. And the human mind is a glutton in its own way, it will eat into whatever you feed it, it has zero sense of filtering the healthy from the junk.

Childhood patterns eventually become traumas that we project on as an adult. Remember Kaira from Dear Zindagi? She found her Jug who helped her heal. I got lucky too when I found my Jug. But it took me many many years before I did. So until you all find your Jug, hoping this helps. You never know you could be someone's Jug some day.

The bicycle example was just one small instance of a pattern, it was not even a trauma. But our unconscious is constantly observing and storing everything. Some people process it better, some need help and it is absolutely okay to ask for help.

I don't know if this has suddenly become a little too heavy. It's probably like Tara touching a nerve in Ved like in the movie Tamasha. I am no Tara, but the point is, we all have that little kid within us who wants our unconditional love, who saw things, experienced things, not knowing how to process and probably kept it to themselves.

You can ask for help only when you identify the problem and acknowledge it. It takes courage to see your own darkness, become vulnerable, accept it without judgement and then seek help.

From *be bitch, not a bichari,* we touched upon some heavy things, but that is how healing and self navigation works.

Activity: This is a safe space. Write down instances when you have felt dark. Think of all the times, when you have felt helpless as if you want to be your best version but something kept pulling you down.

Just let it out. I repeat this is your own safe space.

Activity: This is your *blank* safe space. Write with a pencil and erase it off.

Activity: Don't be in a rush to turn the situation around. Be patient with yourself. Right now we are just letting it out. Cry if you need to. Detoxify.

Activity: Did you think of someone while you were reading and self-reflecting? Someone who hurt you, someone you may have hurt.

Ask yourself if it's worth letting go of the hurt and invite healing for yourself and the person too. Scribble away.

C

Confidence Attracts Opportunities

When making hiring decisions, whether it is in the cricket field or a corporate circus, I have heard people say this quite often. If you want to select between two people; one who is talented and one who is confident, go for the latter.

A talented person who is underconfident and doesn't believe in himself/herself will not only pull himself down but also pull down the team collectively. On the other hand someone who is confident will approach it with a winning mindset and make the process fun.

How to get this confidence is a million dollar question? Are people born confident or can you grow it like a muscle? Does 'fake it till you make it' work? Even I had a dozen questions like this.

Here's what I observed about confident people in my circle.

They are never the ones who know everything. In fact so many times I have been frustrated with my work peers; who knew fairly less about a subject but were able to express, reproduce, shine away with whatever little they knew.

And I always had one or two people around me in every agency I have worked with, who would piss me by doing this. I always lacked confidence despite knowing my shit better than them.

Now when I reflect back, what these people had that I didn't, was, they were all far more easy going in life than me. Confidence often stems from being comfortable with yourself. Confidence also often stems from being comfortable with what you don't know.

See, there are always going to be more things that you don't know than you know, knowledge is like an ocean, you can't possibly know it all. And there will always be someone who will know more than you do.

1. Having clarity about your strengths and weaknesses is the first step in training your confidence muscle.
2. The second step is giving yourself the permission to fail and learn, without being mean to yourself.

If you are a parent reading this; please give your kids permission to make their own mistakes. From your POV you may be protecting them, but what you are really doing is making them handicapped and fearful.

3. The third step is taking action. When you take action, you create a spark between two neurons.

The more you take action, more sparks get generated and the sparks eventually become neural pathways and that is how it becomes effortless. It is a long process, but totally worth it.

Confidence is often directly proportional to how bad you want something. You will see in movies and also in real life, a guy-next-door mustering the courage to talk to a girl way out his league, only because he wants it real bad.

A founder-friend said something to me in this context that has stayed. There is a subtle difference between a big promise and a big bluff. And that is why confident people also end up attracting more opportunities.

They know where and how much to stretch themselves in order to deliver on the big promise, even if they may not have it all figured out. And every person in a certain position of power appreciates this about you because it is how they landed in that position – by taking bets on themselves and building that confidence muscle along the way.

I have often lacked in that area, and was never the most confident person in the room. But I can proudly say that my confidence-meter is far better today, than it was a few years back. There's a long way to go, I am still not the most confident person in the room, but now I know my way around it.

I started content creation a couple of years back with this sole objective of getting better at 'public speaking' or communication skills in general. When I look back on those first videos vs whatever I am creating today, I do have a satisfactory smile.

One more pro-tip. On this journey of becoming a confident version of yourself, you have to be your loudest cheerleader. People will applaud once you finish a race, when they see the end result. Until then, you are alone in the dust and grime, walk, crawl, rest if needed. Slow is fine, stopping isn't, because it's not done until it's done.

Confidence never gets out of style, make it your forever accessory.

Activity: On a scale of 1 to 10, how confident are you according to you.

How would people rate your confidence level?

Recall instances from your childhood when there was no concept of being under confident.

Activity: Recall and write as to when that started changing for you. It could be a silly comment about your color, chubbiness from a relative, could be a remark from a teacher, could be an unappreciated thing from a parent. It could be anything.

Activity: Now ask yourself, if you were the most confident person you know, what would be the first thing you would do. Make a list of things you would do! Start doing it one by one.

D

Don't Ditch the Itch

Fun fact: Ditch the itch was a campaign we had done for an anti-allergy brand back in the agency days. But let me give it a meaningful twist, turn around the perspective.

We often hear people say or even say about people, *"us bande mein bahut khujli hai, full jugadu hai."*

If people have ever said that about you, trust me you are one of those lucky people who have the fire in them. This kind of restlessness is beautiful.

Shah Rukh Khan had once mentioned in an interview that he is jealous of people who don't have this itch, who are happy with how things are. Because when you have the itch, you want to do this, do that, and then you have to push yourself, keep at it, you have to keep stretching it!

For realistic and respectable reasons, some of us may be unable to pursue the itch full time. Like someone who bakes well, may want to do it full time, but has to pay the bills, look after kids, take care of family needs, and then there is only so much time and energy to pursue certain things that itch.

We will talk about balancing it and I am sure some of you are already doing it, we are a hustler generation :)

Did you know that inaction can be more stressful to your body and mind? Because in your mind you are living another life, in reality it's something different. It is going to be stressful, because there is no alignment.

I mean, if stress is unavoidable either way, do it anyway and make the stress worth it.

I also want to break a myth and talk against an otherwise popular opinion that's been shaping our generation these days.

Let's say you are a good painter. People will immediately start pushing you to post it on social media, and run a small business out of it. But believe me at times, it is fine to pursue a hobby just like a hobby, for the fun element without expecting anything else out of it.

We don't always have to have an agenda with our hobbies. Let's express a hobby like a hobby, not a hustle culture. If you feel inside-out that you want to do this full-time, it is a different story. But you decide it from your home frequency, not because someone else wants you to do it.

My parents have been pushing the envelope at sixty, learning all sorts of new things, catering to their itch, with full commitment.

When I told them how proud I am of them, I also expressed a small sorry that they couldn't pursue it before. They took a momentary pause, as if receiving it, acknowledging that they had to prioritize a lot of responsibilities before they could live for themselves. And what they said later, sort of made my eyes wet.

They told me, it may not seem so to me, but that I have been very courageous in giving myself a lot of chances, experimenting with as many career choices here and there before settling in what I genuinely love to do. They said that someone may call it reckless, unfocused, but that it takes guts to choose yourself at times.

I mean to be honest, I did not know I was making bold choices. I was only following my itch because going by the literal meaning of itch, what one can do as a natural response is 'to scratch.' All I did was that.

When I reflect back, I still feel I should have gone all in, scratching it. I still made a lot of choices sitting on the fence, keeping my feet in all boats, instead of failing fast, learning fast.

So, just scratch along homies, the itch is actually the gift.

Activity: Apart from your current job (if you are a working professional reading this), write down 5 things that you like to do that make you happy and fulfilled. It can be just a hobby, it can also be something that can have a business potential too.

1. ______________________________________

____

____

2. ______________________________________

____

____

3. ______________________________________

____

____

4. ______________________________________

____

____

5. ______________________________________

____

____

Activity: Once you have those 5 things in place, research as to who are the people who are at top 3. Stalk them (not literally) follow them on socials, read their Linkedin, study their life story.

This will keep giving you cues about the right direction and the right way to address the itch, from the ones who have already done it.

Thing 1: ________________________________

____

Top 3 in this field: ______________________

____

____

____

____

____

Take away from the research:

____

____

____

____

____

____

____

____

Thing 2: ____________________

Top 3 in this field: ____________________

Take away from the research:

Thing 2: ____________________

Top 3 in this field: ____________________

Take away from the research:

E

Emotional Maturity

Emotions have been my worst enemy until the day I discovered that they can actually be my best friend.

The word emotional intelligence is overused, under understood and has too many contextual interpretations. I myself thought I had a high EI because of how I understood the emotional undercurrents of other people, and got a hang of the emotional energy of the room.

While that could be one of the signs of having a good EI, I want to throw some light on a simpler term; 'emotional maturity' because in my opinion it is more important and realistic.

It's knowing the difference between having emotions and having an emotional drama.

How often do we avoid emotions and call it emotional maturity? How often do we invite emotional drama in the name of emotional intelligence?

Drama happens around an emotion you don't want to deal with, and everyone around you gets pulled in the storm.

While emotional maturity is dealing with it, first by acknowledging its presence without judging yourself and second by deciding what to do with it. If someone pisses you, accept it for yourself, you don't have to go in denial.

After the acceptance, ask yourself what about that person pisses you off, instead of actually lashing out at him/her.

The answer you will get is often a reflection of what you lack within you. Now accepting that is not easy either, the fact that the problem is probably more 'you' than the other person.

When a colleague of mine would piss me off, it was often because I wanted to be confident like her, I would be angry at myself for my own lack of confidence.

There is no easy way to analyse it because it differs a lot from person to person, their learning patterns, their upbringing, their inner talk.

I liked something I read; get ahead of people, don't get even with them.

Let's say your colleague is having a bad day and messes up on some combined task. You both get called in the boss's cabin and have to face the music. Instead of getting even with your colleague and ratting him/her out in front of your boss, you decide to focus on getting the task done.

Taking collective responsibility for the task means getting ahead of the person's fault, and fostering a healthy working relationship. Ofcourse, this doesn't mean you let it pass every time, but you do your best to play the bigger person.

I learnt this from my therapist that, as a human we are always at play with a certain parent-child equation. In any interpersonal relations we are often letting our parent ego be at play or our child ego be a play unless there is emotional maturity.

You may have noticed that age isn't always the benchmark for a person's emotional maturity. There are kids who come across as very mature people while there are some adults who often have child-like behaviour.

In romantic relationships, where two people are mostly equals, it is important that one person doesn't have to face the burden of being a parent all the time. I mean, letting your inner child out and feeling safe in front of your partner is healthy, as long as you both take equal responsibility to be each other's parent.

Women often get labeled as being 'emotional creatures' or often we hear random comments like "Is it that time of the month?" when we lose control of our emotions. So to all men, "if you are saying it out, say it with care and empathy, and not mockery."

A woman has to make more micro-decisions in a day than a man can in an entire month; while juggling the emotional and hormonal changes she undergoes every week. So men show a bit more emotional maturity and help us handle the emotions without making it sound like it is an emotional drama.

Also men have been conditioned growing up to stay strong and not be emotional and hence they find it hard to talk about their feelings. Their feelings are always action oriented, they will do everything they need to be done for their family but when it comes to expressing it in words, in emotional gestures they chicken out.

So as women, we need to learn to navigate them, because what comes naturally to us is a 'men don't do this' zone for them, so we need to be patient, make them feel like we can be their safe space. It's a tough ride but let's start by doing it for our person, change is a gradual thing.

I want to touch upon a sensitive topic here and that is infidelity. Most people don't grow out of love, they grow out of things to say to each other, uncomfortable things, difficult conversations. Most couples avoid it, keep tiptoeing what is meant to be dealt head on and one day one of them happens to find a safe space with some other person, to talk, to cry, to laugh, to express one's mind and that is the downfall of a stable relationship.

There is a great deal to learn about how adults should talk and communicate from Little Things on Netflix and This Is Us on Prime. Top notch recommendations.

Leaving you with a fun quote by Maya Angelou; "Most people don't grow up. They get married, have children, pay bills on time, etc. That's not growing up, that is simply aging. "

So, homies, grow up, don't just age. Don't only be a parent or a child in the relationship, take turns to be the adult too and you will notice for yourself that adulting is not all that bad, you just need a road map for your emotions.

Activity: As a woman reading this, can you recall any recent incident wherein you were only expressing your feeling but the other person dismissed it as an emotional drama. Urge you to share this concept with him/her and clear the air, so that expressing feelings becomes a beautiful task, not a burden.

Activity: As a man reading this, just be observant of all the times, you wanted to share something but suppressed yourself because you were once told as a kid 'boys don't cry'. Write down in the blank space here, if you wish to.

Activity: Do you have something you wanted to tell someone but could not for whatever reason. You either have that person in your life or you don't.

If you are lucky enough to have the person in your life but don't want to reach out, let's say it's an ex, ask yourself was there something you did back you could undo or do better if given a chance. Write it down as if you were undoing it or doing it right.

Cry out a bit if you are feeling heavy, no one's watching, it is a safe space.

Ask for forgiveness, be grateful for the good times and the learning.

Activity: Is there something you want to express to your mother? Complaints, grudges, love, whatever it is, write it down unfiltered. And when you feel a little better call your mom and talk to her for a couple of minutes, just like that.

Activity: Is there something you want to express to your father? Complaints, grudges, love, whatever it is, write it down unfiltered. And when you feel a little better call your dad and talk to him for a couple of minutes, just like that.

Activity: Is there something you want to express to your grandparents? Complaints, grudges, love, whatever it is, write it down unfiltered. And when you feel a little better call them up and chat for a couple of minutes, just like that.

Activity: Is there something you want to express to your brother/sister? Complaints, grudges, love, whatever it is, write it down unfiltered. And when you feel a little better call him/her and chat for a couple of minutes, just like that.

Activity: Is there something you want to express to your friend? Complaints, grudges, love, whatever it is, write it down unfiltered. And when you feel a little better call him/her and chat for a couple of minutes, just like that.

Activity: Is there something you want to express to your girlfriend/boyfriend/husband/wife? Complaints, grudges, love, whatever it is, write it down unfiltered. And when you feel a little better call him/her and chat for a couple of minutes, just like that.

Random activity:

Close your eyes and make a wish.

F

Friends Forever?

When you know to ask the right questions, when you know to be a badass, when you are confident, when you have emotional maturity; when you have all these qualities, which do you think comes handy in making friendships?

None of the above in my opinion. Because most of us don't have any of this inbuilt as kids, and I believe the best of friendships happen when you are naive.

After a certain age – mostly after college, after landing a job, after getting married, after having kids – making friends becomes more and more difficult. What comes at these stages of life are more of symbiotic relations, not those unconditional friendships.

Also, as we grow, some of us evolve into totally different beings than what we used to be in school and college. Our friendships evolve too, we end up feeling disconnected with certain people in the past; maybe more connected with some that we thought we may never bond with.

For some reason, I have come to believe that, after a point in life, it's best to be friends with yourself. I don't mean this in a sad, lonely way.

If you notice people, you will find out that the ones who are extremely content with their own self, ultra comfortable in their own skin, often attract friendships. Because they don't expect a lot from others. Moreover they offer a certain kind of comfort and space to others.

I mean, they themselves may not have articulated it that way as of now; but only when you can be your own best friend, can you be good friends with others. I firmly believe so.

When I started writing this book, I had planned it on the lines of personal branding. That *incident* made me change direction to a great extent. But I would like to explain this with a branding analogy.

Here's a little test on friendship Simon Sinek talks about and I have added my own twist to this from a personal branding lens.

What is a brand? Something that solves a problem for you, most likely far more efficiently and hence has instant recall and recognition.

When I started my career in branding and advertising I was obsessed with the whole, *standing out*, *being different*, *highly competitive*, thing that is typical of branding.

There was a part of me that overlooked humans for humans. It was only their achievements that mattered, that made a human better than another human. And I am sure, I am not the only one, society at large does that.

But something changed after the *incident.*

I still want to believe in the whole branding business, still want to help people build brands and personal brands, but what I also believe now is, what matters is you being better than you, not better than someone else.

Most importantly what matters is, when you go to bed at night, have you been a good human that day. Do you have loved ones with you who cheer for your ups and support you in your downs? Do you have enough private moments that you actually want to hide from social media?

To be truly able to solve problems better and become a remarkable brand, answering all these as YESes is more important.

And to be able to do that you first got to be your own best friend. Because, we are never hard on our friends and are full of life advice, full of support. Then why deny yourself that, become your own best friend.

I have been envious of people for whom friendships came easy and all my life I have tried to fit into groups but never could, always felt like an outsider. If you are like me, here are two solutions, either of these will work for you.

1. First just be comfortable with who you are in your own skin. Only then you will find your own tribe, your own group. Start slow, start small, attract people that suit your vibe.

2. Second thing (which applies to me) is the idea that a group or tribe may really not be for you (it's something we start admiring because of movies). I am in love with the idea of having 'a best friend' over calling every third person a 'bestie' – the smaller the circle the more sacred it is.

I am more of a Jai-Veeru person than a ZNMD person. (I know too many Bollywood references. I don't know how to explain these to non-Indian people!)

Choose to enjoy your own company over settling down with a group of friends that don't match your vibe, the right ones will come along when you first make space for yourself.

Activity: Pick 10 names and seed this question in a random, candid conversation – *give me 3 reasons we are friends.*

5 of whom you consider your close friend.

5 of whom consider you their close friend.

They are going to get caught off-guard and may want to casually skip the question; but I leave it up to your skill set and equation with the person how to get your answers.

Write them down. DM me @themerakiwoman in case you would like to discuss what their comments translate to.

- ______________________________
  ____
- ______________________________
  ____
- ______________________________
  ____
- ______________________________
  ____
- ______________________________
  ____
- ______________________________
  ____

Activity: Do you agree with their answers? If yes, why? If not, why?

What according to you makes you a good friend. Write write write.

Random activity:

Write about the person you were thinking of right before you opened this page.

G

Gratitude is Growth

It's this one thing, that is hands down directly proportional to who you turn out to be – bitter or better.

I mean, every other thing I have mentioned so far can have varying intensities depending on who is reading, how it's being understood and received, how it's being applied – it could be subject to individual interpretations to an extent. But gratitude is the constant to these variables.

The more grateful you are about what you have, the more of it you will have.

And I want to bring some clarity to this concept, because just like manifestation, most of us have been practising gratitude the wrong way.

Being grateful doesn't mean 'visualizing being happy and grateful as your wishes come true.'

I am not asking you to 'visualize' being grateful. You aim for a brand-new car – you imagine with your thoughts, feelings that you have the car already and feel grateful about it.

That's not how gratitude works at the fundamental level. At the core of it, gratitude means – feeling thankful for the car that you currently have – feeling it with all the genuineness you can possibly muster – thinking about all the amazing moments you could experience because of that existing car, only because of that car – being thankful that maybe if it wasn't for that car – your dog could not have survived that accident or you wouldn't have bonded with your friend over deep conversations over long drives etc.

The way gratitude functions is letting the Universe, the Force, Whoever you have fully surrendered to, know how much you appreciate what you have in the moment because there could be so many who dream of having what you have – the health you have, the parents you have, the job you have, the friends you have, that gift of painting/singing that you have, that latest i-phone you so casually own, that movie date you have, the clean water you casually use, the tiffin your mom packs for you, the first mango of the season your father gets for you, the loved one at home who waits for you.

I know people who have turned around their lives, by simply acknowledging how grateful they are for their existing gifts.

I am not really the most fun person I know, I have been pretty serious about things all my life. Trust me, it hasn't helped me at all. It's not that I was ungrateful for my gifts, but my gratitude prayer always ended with a 'but' – like I am grateful for so & so, but I am sad about so & so.

Life has weird ways of teaching you lessons. There was this one time when I went through a bad hospitalisation, I had grown so weak that my smile looked scary, I was losing hair like a chemo patient. That's when I realised I never received all the compliments people used to give me about my smile or looks. I was not being rude about the compliments, just that I took it for granted, thinking 'what is the big deal' there are far more prettier faces. Just remember that what you have is indeed precious, the sooner you realise the better.

While I know the reality of this theory, let me be honest with you, I have tough days when the feeling of despair is far more stronger than the feeling of gratitude. I am yet to fully achieve that state myself.

I guess practising gratitude is not like building a muscle where you hit the gym for a couple of hours and tadaaa you have it!

It's more like meditation, you have to keep being mindful of it every second and considering the monkey mind and its wavering nature, it's hard, I admit. But one day at a time, one mindful breath at a time, I believe it will come naturally to me sooner or later.

Gratitude is also different from being hopeful or seeing positives in negatives. I hate the glass half full half empty analogy. Gratitude is being mindful of the water in glass, the thirst it will quench. It's believing that you won't go thirsty. It's also about offering some of the water to someone thirstier than you when you have extra water. It's knowing that at the end of the day you are only a vessel, a medium and water like grace is free flowing.

Activity: So as to get better at it and so that it's on autopilot mode, I have recently started maintaining a daily gratitude diary. I write a couple of pages about all the good things that happened that day, sometimes it is about some past happy memories with loved ones, and a general reflection about life.

It is helping me. It will help you too.

Start with 10 things you are grateful for at this very moment in your life. Don't overthink, just go with the flow, write.

1. ______________________________

____

2. ______________________________

____

3. ______________________________

____

4. ______________________________

____

5. ______________________________

____

6. ______________________________

____

7. ______________________________

____

8. ____

____

9. ____

____

10. ____

____

Activity: List of things you are grateful for in this year.

1. ______________________________
____

2. ______________________________
____

3. ______________________________
____

4. ______________________________
____

5. ______________________________
____

6. ______________________________
____

7. ______________________________
____

8. ______________________________
____

9. ______________________________
____

10. ______________________________
____

H

Humor Me

I must have been in college when I stumbled upon a surprising fact about Charlie Chaplin, the comedian who could make the world laugh with just a tilt of his hat or a shuffle of his feet. Beneath the laughter, Chaplin lived a life full of sadness. Yet, he chose to create humor, both for himself and the world around him. That revelation left an indelible mark on me: humor is not the absence of sadness but a brave choice to find light even in the darkest corners.

Studies show that people who can crack a joke or two as a part of casual conversations; have witty comebacks score higher on intelligence and emotional maturity. Their neural pathways are healthier, they are good at problem solving and they are fast learners. A sense of humor is more likely to build stronger relationships, overcome challenges, and even improve health. When we take life too seriously, we trap ourselves in a cycle of worry and stress.

To be very honest with you; I suck at it too. I am the most serious person I know and move around as if *'duniya ka bojha mere kandhon pe hai'*

I have literally googled what I am about to share with you now and I am teaching myself to do this too. Few realistic hacks to help you (and me) to make friends with 'humor'

1. Schedule a 'silly time'

   Watch comedy shows, funny animal videos, sing a song like no one's hearing, dance like no one's watching.

2. Set a 'silly alarm on your phone'

   Schedule random reminders during the day with funny messages: *"Have you smiled today, you glorious overthinker?"*

3. Practice the "Pause, Laugh, Move On" Rule

   When you overthink something, pause and ask yourself, "Is this funny now or will it be funny later?" If it will be funny later, don's fuss about it; laugh and move on.

4. End the Day with a Humor Habit

   Before bed, think of one funny thing that happened during the day. If nothing stands out, make one up! This ritual helps you focus on joy before sleep.

If you learn about more such hacks or you invent some of your own, please share it with me too.

If life gives you lemons, squeeze some on your (sad) life and make it fresh and citrusy! (lol, lame, maybe, but I kinda smiled)

Activity: (Just a blank page for random blabbers)

I

I am the Universe, *Aham Brahmasmi*

'I' is like a double edged sword. Too much of it is ego, too less of it is lack of self esteem, the right amount is self-respect.

We all know what *aham brahmasmi* means. But we keep forgetting it and don't really follow or apply it in real life. This gives birth to man-made gods in every nook and corner. We just give away the power to some third entity.

Despite having a lot of questions about God and struggling to find my faith in one God (because Hinduism has many gods) I have been a blind believer in the concept of God all my life, and too much of anything is bad.

When I did a course on transactional analysis, one of the modalities of psychotherapy, one realisation was very stark. We were asked to do one activity – recall some of your childhood memories and discuss with your respective group.

The most prominent ones that sprung in my memory lane were stories that mom told me. When I did my own analysis I realised that all the stories that I recalled had characters waiting on someone to rescue them from something. There were other stories too but these had a sharper recall and I wondered if I was aping the stories, waiting for someone to rescue me.

It made me question a lot of things about how my belief system was shaped. I believe that is the case with a lot of us – we are all waiting on someone for something to happen. We are all god-fearing people, doing so called rights only because we know someone up there is watching, and the consequences scare us; we rarely do the kind of right that feels right.

Despite us all knowing *aham brahmasmi* we are all too busy doing things for the universe that lies outside of us, and by that I mean social constructs, instead of pulling back the power to us, to the universe within.

Sadhguru describes Shiva as the AdiYogi, the first one to come into 'yog' state that is a state of union with his inner universe and outer universe. Instead of learning this aspect we are all about *Shiv ji ko bel chadhao or jal chadao etc.*These rituals are symbolic of something deep but we are too chaotic about even trying to understand what it stands for. Bel is symbolic of any wild leaf, meaning anything you offer with devotion, God will accept it, because who are we to really offer anything to God in the first place!

I may be coming from a place of loss and grief due to the recent *incident*; but *aham brahmasmi* helps to reduce dependency on other people, other entities. You start to expect more from yourself than from others. I believe the day you start doing this, it will be half the battle won. But watch out for anything becoming 'too much' – too much I or *aham* can be ego. There is a power beyond us. Moderation is the key.

Carl Jung says, "The one who sees outside, dreams. The one who sees within, awakens."

To be able to navigate yourself, you must trust your inner GPS. To be able to find out what is meant for you, you must start listening. Prayers means you talk to the Divine and Meditation means you listen to the Divine. Seek balance between both.

There's one more thing I would like to highlight, not exactly related to the topic, but important in the context of any topic or any dream to take shape and that is this one liner – inaction is the root cause of all stress.

You learn all the theory in the world, unless and until you action it, it is practically useless.

I am a procrastinator myself and there are days when I find it very difficult to take action on anything and those are the exact same days when I am in the worst states of mental despair and self-doubt.

You can have best of resources in the world, but no one can push for you – the right sports gear, the right athleisure, a nice running track, great community – but if you keep snoozing the alarm, you are not going to get fit – you can't hire someone else to run on your behalf and get fit – no technology can make this possible – you have to push for yourself.

Activity: Write down 10 times "I am the Universe". *aham brahmasmi.*

Activity: Write down "I am…" affirmations for yourself.

- ____
  ____
- ____
  ____
- ____
  ____
- ____
  ____
- ____
  ____
- ____
  ____
- ____
  ____
- ____
  ____
- ____
  ____
- ____
  ____

J

Just Do It – a Game of Narrations and Perspectives

Being in the profession of branding and advertising; I have always been drawn to how brands come with interesting campaigns, how they weave their purpose statements so tight with their taglines and so on.

No prizes for guessing that 'Just Do It' by Nike is one of the legendary taglines that everyone in branding considers a benchmark. And if you don't know the backstory, just google about Simon Sinek's Ted Talk on what Phil Knight would speak about 'Just Do It'

I am here to share a new piece of information I discovered about the origin of this tagline that blew my mind and made me believe more in the power of storytelling and how a story's narrative can be a game changer.

But before you read further, please check out the above mentioned video by Simon Sinek; only then will you be able to put things into perspective, about what I am not going to share.

Just Do It were actually the last words uttered by a convict to the firing squad just before he was executed. Dan Wieden, the creative brain behind Nike's campaign, gave it the most legendary spin to three random words, and spun around a timeless tagline out of it.

Dan Wieden believed that rules are meant to be broken, and it was this playful philosophy that made his agency the most sought out back in the 70's.

The point I am trying to make here is: if you are open and observant about things, ideas and inspiration will fall into your lap. Thereafter, it is about what you believe in and how you can manifest, reinvent and make a better reality for you.

I consider myself the most non-judgemental person I know and almost everyone who knows me personally will agree to this.

I am grateful that this makes me very open to perspectives and sometimes even I am amazed at how solutions come looking for me.

I don't know if one is born with this quality or one can also develop it like a muscle, just like we spoke about building confidence.

I haven't googled on how to develop this quality, but reflecting back on my childhood days here's what must have helped.

Stories.

"Stories, as it turns out, were crucial to our evolution more so than opposable thumbs. Opposable thumbs, let us hang on; stories told us what to hang on to." Lisa Cron

I was really into it, thanks to my parents.

My mom used to narrate one story to me every single day, and I mean it every single day before going to bed – everything from Shivaji Maharaj to Ramayana Mahabharata, to the traditional Panchatantra.

Many times the stories were her own creations, some from her own childhood, narrated as is and sometimes narrated with reinvented versions blended with imaginations.

My dad used to get books for me, my first reading memories go back to Champak, Gokulam, Reader's Digest. Later on upgrading to Nancy Drew, Hardy boys and then graduating to Sydney Sheldon, Dan Brown and what not in college.

Travel is another great way to get a hang on perspectives. Piyush Pandey, India's legendary adman, considers traveling (especially across the country) his greatest source of inspiration whenever he comes up with iconic campaigns. That is because Bharat as a country changes so much every mile, right from what we speak, eat, think, get influenced – there's no better and simpler way to broaden your perspectives than to travel the country.

Jagriti Yatra is a great initiative in this direction. It is a 15 day train journey across the country that enables young entrepreneurs to connect with each other. The forms are usually out by the end of December every year.

Perspectives come in handy while navigating yourself because it helps you look at yourself outside of a set template, it gives you the flexibility, adaptability to play your own game, be your own timeline and keep becoming your authentic self.

Activity: Any stories that you remember particularly about your childhood? Select one and give it different perspectives. Give your imagination a free hand.

K

Karma Won't Be a Bitch Unless You Are

What I am about to say, could be a little advanced for some of you or not for some of you.

There are times in life, when you end up doing things, that you literally warn yourself to stay away from. Feels like there are some forces above you making you do those things; feels helpless. Most often these involve people – exes, bosses, siblings, even parents and spouses. Makes you want to go back in time and right some wrongs if you were ever given a chance. Been there?

Believe me or not, these are karmic connections, rather karmic debts that you are here on earth to pay back. They say, you don't choose your family, you only choose your friends. That is not entirely true. Do you think it is random that you are born to a particular set of parents? You have most certainly chosen that at a soul-level and so have your parents chosen you, or that particular soul, because of a pending transaction, or karmic connection.

Be very mindful of your intentions. Although it is very important for your actions to align with your intentions, just be constantly aware of your intentions, because as they say in Bhagavad Gita *'karta karavita toh ahe'* – the act and the doer of the act is GOD himself, you are just a vessel. Do your very best to be a *good vessel.*

Every law of physics has its roots in the Bhagavad Gita. I would like to share one that feels personal to me; here goes:

Newton's Second Law: The acceleration of an object is directly proportional to the net force acting on it and inversely proportional to its mass.

Bhagavad Gita: In the Bhagavad Gita, Krishna suggests selflessness in actions, or the dissolution of ego (I, me, myself), which can be considered our internal or psychological "mass." If we minimize this ego and align our intent with the values of the universe, our acceleration towards spiritual growth could be immense, approaching infinity.

Spiritual Growth: The corollary here is that just as reducing mass increases acceleration (given a constant force), minimizing ego can lead to rapid spiritual advancement.

You will be surprised to know how the laws of karma and Newtonian physics draw parallels from one another. I sometimes wonder if Krishna and Newton were the same person; same soul, different bodies, different eras.

So the takeaway is to navigate yourself with intentions of personal growth and not to avenge someone, show superiority or anything of that sort.

Activity: Do some research on how Newton's 1st law and 2nd law of physics can be weaved back in the law of karma as stated in the Bhagavad Gita.

L

Leadership Means to Fail in One Direction Only

Is leadership a skill set you are born with? You see some kids who are very outgoing, they take to the stage, aren't shy at all, and won't hesitate to start a conversation. Most often they also end up taking leadership positions as adults.

But we also come across people who turned leaders because life gave them no other choice. It was either step up or perish. Kung Fu Panda is a classic example of how leadership qualities were invoked in him.

There's an entire training industry thriving on 'making leaders' out of you. Ever been to such sessions? I mean they aren't bad; but how many of them make Kung Fu Pandas?

If you have ever been in close proximity of a real leader (not a wanna be leader) you will find the dormant leader within you awakening. That is what a true leader does – create more leaders, not more followers.

I know someone, who ignited this within me, but the saddest part is he isn't around in the physical realm to read this, he was and will always be my best friend, who taught me by example that leadership is the ability to believe in people and give them the confidence that, they can win every single day.

I believe a true leader is no less than a guru; and if you can surrender to him/her, your life starts finding and living its purpose on its own.

Leadership isn't always a roaring loud clear voice within you. At times, it is the humble, curious, figuring-out, voice too. So don't question yourself if you can't take up to stage and deliver a sweet talk. Here are some telltale signs to find if you have true leadership qualities.

- You operate from a position of humility and power; always ready to give, ready to help but it's far from being desperate to help. (I have made this mistake of being desperate to help maybe because it was satisfying some complex within me)
- You are equally willing to receive help with dignity, without the slightest bit of complex or agitation, because for you the end objective is more important
- You are emotionally mature, you know the difference between having emotions and creating emotional drama

Can you build this up as a muscle, practise the above points? The answer is Yes & No. Because if you try too hard, you may come across as a wannabe.

More importantly, being a leader is not like going to the gym consistently. It's more like going to the gym and people taking a note of you, feeling inspired to join the gym too. People need to accept you as the leader; only then the collective change will be a compound effect.

He told me something when I was going through a phase. "Fail in one direction, that's how you build an empire."

The context to this was the original idea of the book, called find your superpower. Given our individual journeys in our career, we had drawn certain conclusions about types of people.

- Who know right from the start, what they want, stick to it, pursue it, succeed at it
- Who know from the start, what they want, but end up doing something entirely different
- Who don't know what they want, need to explore a lot of things and learn hands on where they would like to excel

He was a mix of the first two and I was a mix of the last two. And during one such time when I kept exploring instead of consolidating, he gave that 'fail in one direction' nugget. What he meant was, only people who have failed a lot and failed in a certain direction, know the ins and outs of that process, they have stuck to the same path because they enjoy the process of building, and any person with this mindset has leadership abilities whether they know it or not, whether people recognise it yet or not. And for people to recognize the leader in you, you have to recognise it first, feed it first. The lion is the king of the jungle because he believes he is the king of the jungle. It is as simple and as difficult as that.

Don't keep waiting to be discovered because maybe someone is waiting for you to discover them. Just start living life, one day at a time, as your fullest expression.

Activity: Do you consider yourself a leader? If yes, why? If not, what is that one thing that is stopping you?

Random activity:

Think of a person you want to punch in the face, create a lame joke around him/her, laugh it out (don't go and punch for real!)

M

Meraki is the Way

I have been obsessed with this word ever since I discovered it.

It is a Greek word which means, doing everything that you do with your heart, soul and creativity into it; leaving a piece of you in your work.

I had this good and bad habit that I would not take up any task unless I felt like, unless it felt from within. Example: I had to write 10 pages a day, I would do it only if it felt like, because I had this thing that; it has to be inside out or else it not will be my 100%

And that was a mistake I made. I chose talent over consistency.

Wanting to be authentic and wanting to live a life of meraki is a great desire to have. I used to be so proud of myself as a kid for having big dreams and big plans. I am sure all of us relate to this. We ourselves are responsible for the growing gaps between our dreams and reality.

I wish I knew before that consistency is the foundation of building authenticity. The more you do, the more you get polished, the more you get polished, the diamond within you shines.

I was in this dilemma all my life – whether you choose or whether you are chosen.

The simple-complex answer is, you have to choose first, keep choosing, if you are on the path you are meant to be, life won't pull you out; but if it does pull you out from that path, something beyond your control happens, assure yourself that it wasn't the path for you. Tune back your frequencies and start walking on the new path life has put you on.

At times, when I am lost and confused, feeling demotivated, I sort of chant this word, it's like my personal-mantra. Sort of use it to shift from the state of self-doubt to the present state.

Just like I have a personal code word, I also feel that me-time is ultra sacred. It helps you create healthy gaps between triggers and actions; so that your actions come from an authentic place and not a triggered place.

I break down my me-time into slots of planned me-time and unplanned me-time.

Planned slots are usually early mornings and late nights just before going to bed. Activities mainly include – meditation, journaling, mantra chanting.

Unplanned slots are during the day when things become a bit overwhelming – quick walks, listening to music, watching movies and something I recently started is revisiting photos of your loved ones in your phone gallery.

For those of you who have a question on how to meditate; I would recommend Vipassana; it will guide you to a great deal on the art of connecting with your authentic self.

My Vipassana teacher explains it as an open surgery you perform on your mind, to cleanse it; so it will hurt, but that is also the way you heal.

Activity: What does your me-time comprise of?

Activity: Any random thoughts you would like to pen down? Go right ahead.

N

NO means a YES to Things You Deeply Care About

My childhood friend shared something shocking after I casually discussed the book with her.

She didn't even know she was struggling with 'validation' until one day it was almost about to sabotage her corporate career.

She is currently at a mid management position and she ensures that she treats her colleagues the way she would have wanted others to treat her back when she was new.

She told me, "I would go about saying Yes to everything anyone asked of me, sometimes even at the cost of compromising my morals and ethics. Ya, I was weak. Not weak in character, but weak in courage. I could just not stand up for what I felt was right."

Many of us face this, right? Saying NO comes with difficulty. I have myself faced this so often. And everyone has different reasons. Sometimes, you are trying hard to belong. Sometimes, you feel you are an imposter and always feel you are doing less. Sometimes, it's competition with colleagues, the desperation to impress.

Sometimes, you don't know what to say NO to, only because you don't have a strong goal to focus on. And this is very different from the above scenarios. Here you are probably making a conscious choice to explore a lot of options, maybe a lot of internships.

I came across a TED Talk by Justine Musk. She shared a profound insight into Elon Musk's decision-making process: he says "No" a lot. Behind every firm "No" lies a deeper "Yes" to what truly matters. This resonated deeply with me. When you lose your "deep Yes" – your authenticity – you also lose the ability to say a strong, intentional "No."

I know this first hand because, for a phase of my life, I was constantly saying "Yes" to things that didn't serve me and "No" to things that would've aligned with my true self. It was chaotic, disorienting, and exhausting. One day, I hit a breaking point and decided that something had to change.

I packed my bags and went for a Vipassana retreat. I disconnected from the world, logging off to reset my inner "feed" much like a digital detox, but for the soul. It wasn't just a one-time thing; it became a practice I revisited periodically to break patterns of saying "Yes" to the wrong things.

For almost a year after that, I was unrecognizable to those around me. Family functions? Skipped. Social obligations? Declined. Conversations that drained me? Ghosted.

This intentional phase of saying “No” to everything had its consequences. People called me stubborn, unapproachable, even selfish. But deep down, I knew this was the labor pain of rediscovering my authentic self.

Activity: Are you a Yes person? What makes you one? List down the probable reasons.

Activity: List down the places (at work, at home) and people (friends, parents, bosses, partners, exes) that you can't say NO to.

Activity: Choose one thing you do simply to please someone else, and commit to saying NO to it from today onward. As you make that decision, remind yourself: "I am embracing the Power of NO to align with my deeper YES and connect to my authentic frequency."

Pro-tips to politely say No, and a deeper YES to what really matters:

- **I appreciate the offer, but I'll have to pass this time**
- **Thank you for thinking of me, but I'm unable to commit right now**
- **I'm honored by the invitation, but I have other commitments**
- **Unfortunately, I won't be able to help with that, but I appreciate the opportunity**
- **This isn't the right fit for me at the moment, but I hope we can work together in the future**
- **I'm flattered by the request, but I have to decline.**
- **I have to prioritize other responsibilities, so I can't take this on**
- **I've given it some thought, and I've decided it's not something I can take on right now**
- **I'm not able to say yes to this, but thank you for understanding**
- **This isn't something I'm able to do at the moment, but I really appreciate the thought**

Random activity:

Draw your spirit animal (in whatever poor drawing capacity). If you don't have a spirit animal, draw your favorite, bird, reptile, animal.

O

One Thing You Would Do If…

1. If you had only a year to achieve it?

2. If you knew the outcome was guaranteed?

3. If you had to take a small first step today?

4. If you weren't afraid of failing?

5. If you had to be completely honest with yourself?

6. If you wanted to take a step closer to your ideal self?

7. If you trusted yourself more?

8. If you stopped chasing perfection?

8. If you stopped comparing yourself to others?

P

Pressure of Having it All by 30

We are a generation of hustlers. We want everything and we want it fast. It's not a bad thing or a good thing. The only thing to remember here is, don't succumb to the pressure because of how good others are doing. Do it because the authentic you has a dream.

While chasing a particular dream, if you ignore other important aspects like health and relationships, success will have to sooner or later slow down. Not having the health to enjoy the wealth, not having your loved ones to share your success with, isn't exactly success.

How much ever I say this, how much anyone says anything about this, it is only some bitter personal experience that will suddenly make you want to take corrective steps.

So ya, it's the shortest of all our topical conversations.

Activity: Google 'wheel of success'. You will find a pie chart with 5-6 pie namely – career, health, family, friends, spirituality, personal growth.

Draw it here. Mark your strongest to weakest area. Take corrective measures accordingly.

Q

Quintessential

Make your own navigation tool from this word…

R

Real Question: What Do You Want Right Now?

Here's the thing – there's no rulebook. What you want right now doesn't have to look like what others want. Your path may be unconventional, and that's totally fine. Forget the expectations. The only question that matters is: What do YOU want to do today?

If you're uncertain about the next step, start small:

- **What excites you today?**
- **What brings you peace?**
- **What would you do if there were no limitations?**

You have your whole life ahead of you. So, stop worrying about the "ideal" timeline and trust that the path will unfold in its own time. The key is to show up, do the work, and keep asking: What's next?

Activity: What's your 'right now?' What's your 'what's next?'

S

Self-Love or Self-Sabotage?

A friend of mine orders herself food every time something goes right or wrong for her. It's her way of coping with things or rewarding herself for small achievements.

She lives with her parents, there's no pressure of supporting the family with the money she earns. Her monthly food delivery bills are anywhere between 30k-40k and she calls this 'self-love.'

When I told her she needed to watch what she was doing to her body (as she had put on unhealthy amounts of weight), she asked me not to body-shame her.

Self-love as a concept is often misconstrued.

Committing to self-love, doesn't mean you treat yourself like a child whom you never want to scold and cater to that child's every whim and fancy. It also doesn't mean reprimanding the child at the slightest mischief; so as to discipline him.

Self-love means you are patient and empathetic with yourself; it means you give yourself the permission to make mistakes and most importantly to learn from them.

Committing to self-love is not like the 'happily ever after' signage they show in movies after the couple gets married. It is in fact what happens each day after marriage.

It's also not like one day you commit to it, shower yourself with all the love, empathy and patience and the next day you will be all flawless and perfect. It just means that you take effort in the direction of becoming a better version of yourself.

You give yourself as many chances as you need and make persistent consistent effort, because self-love takes courage and the lines often get blurry.

Louise Hay says, "Until you love yourself, you will never know who you really are and you won't know what you are capable of."

I felt what she meant. Do you really love yourself wholly? Most of us only love the light in us, we reject and abandon our own dark. It's like you just love one side of the coin, when both sides make the whole coin.

Take a moment to ponder the depth of her lines.

Activity: List down things you love about yourself.

Activity: List down things you hate about yourself.

Activity: Did someone say something to you that made you love something about yourself or hate something about yourself. Just ponder and write.

Activity: Any chance you have said something to someone that may have resulted in loving themselves for it or hating themselves for it. Just ponder, write, be mindful about it the next time.

Activity: Write and affirm "I love myself unconditionally, with all the light and dark."

T

Timeline, Not Deadline

Meeting deadlines and setting stricter ones next time has its own thrill. The sense of achievement that comes with ticking tasks off a list is undeniably nice. But let us not become mere puppets chasing deadlines for the sake of it. Life is not a deadline – it's your own beautiful timeline.

Every person has a unique equation with time. We often say things like *mera time acha chal raha hai* or *mera time bura chal raha hai*, casually attributing our fortunes to time itself. These statements often arise when we compare our journeys with others, leaving us stuck and unhappy. However, when we pause and reflect, the happiest memories tend to come from enjoying the process, the people, and the experiences along the way – not just reaching the destination.

One of my favorite life lessons comes from a Bollywood film: *"Simple hai, kuch logon ke sath sirf waqt bitane se sab kuch sahi ho jata hai."* Who you spend your time with is crucial because people's energies influence you more than you realize. Finding the right people often comes after encountering a few wrong ones – but that's part of the process.

On the other hand, many of us plan far into the future, often at the expense of the present. Abraham Lincoln wisely said, *"The best thing about the future is that it comes one day at a time."* Life is fragile and unpredictable. Cherish the present – every cup of tea, every conversation, every picture you click, every text, every little thing with a loved one – because you never know which might be the last.

Time is free but priceless. You can't own it, but you can use it. You can't keep it, but you can spend it wisely. It's not about being early or late – it's about being on time, on *your* time.

Timing and decision-making go hand in hand, shaping how you take charge of your life. In a professional setting, we often encounter people who are either too impatient or too slow. Navigating such work dynamics requires prioritization and adaptability.

Start by making small but meaningful changes – like honoring your verbal commitments and showing up on time. These small habits create a powerful ripple effect, helping you build a healthier relationship with time.

Life isn't about racing against the clock – it's about flowing with it, embracing every moment with intention and grace.

Sharing a few questions, to first understand your own equation with time and then to better it.

Activity:

1. What feels "on time" or "off track" in your life right now?

   ____

   ____

   ____

   ____

   ____

   ____

2. Are you currently where you thought you would be at this stage in life? Yes/No. Why?

   ____

   ____

   ____

   ____

   ____

3. How aware are you of your daily, weekly, or yearly progress toward my goals?

   ____

   ____

   ____

   ____

   ____

4. How do you define "good timing" in your life?

____

____

____

____

5. Do you struggle to balance waiting for the "right time" versus taking action now?

____

____

____

____

6. How do you cope when life doesn't go according to your timeline?

____

____

____

____

7. Are there instances when life's timing worked out better than you could have planned?

____

____

____

____

Activity: Ponder more on the above activity if you may like.

U

Understanding Your Inner Voice

We all have that internal monologue – the dialogue that runs in our heads when things don't go as planned, when we make mistakes, or when we don't meet our own expectations.

For many years, I struggled with this self-dialogue. It wasn't a supportive voice; rather, it was one filled with criticism and doubt.

This experience led me to ask an important question to many people:

What's your self-dialogue like when you make a mistake or don't fulfill an expectation?

Here's what I discovered about the types of self-dialogues people usually have.

- **A Healthy Self-Dialogue: People who respond to mistakes with compassion, seeing them as opportunities for growth.**
- **A Toxic Self-Dialogue: Those who are overly critical, leading to self-sabotage and even a feeling of paralysis.**
- **A Misunderstood Self-Dialogue: A twist on the idea of being kind to yourself, but still**

using unhealthy methods of coping, like overeating or overindulging.

- **A Masked Dialogue: Assertiveness in public or with others but sabotage or self-blame in private.**

Where will you place yourself?

Whatever is your type, the universe will play by its rule of being the mirror.

It will reflect the energy you put into it. If you're desperate, if you're chasing success with a hunger that feels like it will consume you, the universe picks up on that.

Desperation is a frantic energy, a vibration that says, "I need this now, or I'll lose everything." And when you approach your journey with desperation, you actually push away the very things you're seeking. It's like trying to force a door open – no matter how much you pull, you can't get in until the door opens at the right time.

Now, think of the alternative: curiosity. Curiosity is an open, inviting energy. It says, "I'm not sure where this path will lead, but I'm eager to explore." It's like being a child in a vast museum – you don't rush from one exhibit to the next, desperate to see it all.

Instead, you linger, you look closer, you ask questions, you soak it all in. When you're curious, you stop stressing about the destination and allow the journey to unfold naturally. You let the universe guide you because you trust that it will bring you exactly what you need, when you need it.

Activity:

1. How often do you notice your inner voice during the day?

 ____

 ____

 ____

 ____

 ____

2. What triggers negative self-talk in you?

 ____

 ____

 ____

 ____

 ____

3. When was the last time you forgave yourself for something you couldn't control?

 ____

 ____

 ____

 ____

 ____

4. When was the last time you showered yourself with unconditional love?

____

____

____

____

____

5. How do you respond to constructive criticism – from yourself and others?

____

____

____

____

____

Activity: Ponder more on the above activity if you may like.

V

Vipassana, a Way of Life

Vipassana means seeing things the way they are.

We often glorify someone we like or belittle someone we don't. A lot of things we do have biases of likes and dislikes. This snatches away the power of seeing things the way they are. It traps us in a cycle of action, reaction and thus the karmic give and take of life.

The more we are able to dissociate from likes and dislikes, the more likely we are to free ourselves from this cycle and achieve moksha. That is the teaching of Vipassana, a meditation technique that originates from Buddhism.

Few of my relatives mocked me when I did it for the first time. Told me, people do such things in old age. But I did it nevertheless because I was aware of how much I needed it, to calm my mind, to train my mind to dissociate.

The less I say about it the better, because it is something every young and old must experience not just once but every now and then.

Activity: Sit with yourself for 15 minutes, doing nothing.

W

What You Seek is Seeking You…

Life often mirrors our inner desires. What you deeply seek has a way of finding you.

This doesn't mean sitting back and simply waiting; it means being intentional, persistent, and open to possibilities.

However, in this pursuit, not every challenge is worth your energy. Some battles drain you more than they serve you. Winning every argument, proving every point, or chasing everything you want can leave you depleted.

Choosing your battles wisely means understanding where your energy creates meaningful impact. Seek what aligns with your values, passions, and purpose. Let go of what only feeds ego or insecurity. In doing so, you don't just attract what you seek – you become ready to receive it with clarity and strength.

While following *what you seek is seeking you*, I believe it is important that it comes from a place of your home frequency, a sense of clarity about whether your desires are really yours.

Similarly when picking up the right battles, there will come a point wherein you could be confused about whether or not it is the right battle for you. The cue here is energy. How does it feel – depleted or driven?

Activity: Write down your deepest desires with your non-dominant hand (left hand) in most cases.

XZY...

We often use *xyz* as phrases as fillers – continuations of thoughts, placeholders for what's left unsaid, or a way to trail off with an implied "etc." But life, unlike words, doesn't allow us to drift in ambiguity for long.

When I began writing this book a few months ago, what started as one idea evolved into something deeper. As I rewrote and reflected, my belief system shifted from one polarity to another – a transformation I didn't see coming.

Living in extremes isn't easy. You either carve your name into history or find yourself learning from mistakes that feel monumental in the moment. Both paths demand courage.

Whether you choose the intensity of extremes or the steadiness of moderation, let it be *your* choice – one made with intention, not fear. Follow it with conviction, without regrets, and see it through. After all, life isn't about avoiding missteps – it's about embracing the journey, and reaching where you are meant to.

Activity: Write about your favourite A to Z navigator tool

Activity: Make your own A to Z navigator tool

Activity: Make your own A to Z navigator tool

Activity: Make your own A to Z navigator tool

Activity: Make your own A to Z navigator tool

Activity: Make your own A to Z navigator tool

Activity: Since you have randomly opened this page, it is a sign for you to slow down, remember to breathe before you begin again.

This second part of the book is a bunch of questions you need to ask yourself, that will help you arrive at your calling, sooner in life.

I have my few cents on it. Would love to know your take on them. You know where to find me, right. Insta handle **the meraki woman**

Find Your Superpower

The original idea for penning down this book was to help you *find your superpower.*

Sumedh & I had coined a new meaning for the word, superpower, as the combination of two skill sets – tangible and intangible that make you good at what you are. Sometimes we know it consciously, sometimes we don't.

So, the whole idea was to identify it, give it a conscious structure so that we find our calling sooner in life and live a fulfilled happy life.

He had interacted with different people as a young entrepreneur, who had a successful agency up and running for six years at 27.

I had interacted with different people as a corporate person working with agencies and also on the client side, but as someone who kept jumping places every two-three years, in search of something more fulfilling till I was 35.

That's why we both agreed that there are primarily two types of people in a work set up – people like him who get it right, right from the start, who choose to fail and build in one direction and then there were people like me who had to take a longer route to arrive at failing and building in one direction.

That is how we conceived the idea for this book, and came up with a simple formula of sorts. We call it the superpower, a combination of two skill sets, because what we noticed from our interactions with people is that those who make it big often have a combination of these two.

Example: Sumedh had excellent data skills (tangible) and excellent people skills (intangible) and that is what made him what he was.

I identified this for me, after we cracked the formula. Tangible (words) and intangible (perspectives).

In the very first attempt, you may arrive at two or more words for each skill set, and that is fine; eventually you will arrive at a more sharper version.

Sharing a few questions, for you to ponder on and write the answers:

- **What would you do with your time if you never had to worry about money?**

  ____

  ____

  ____

  ____

  ____

  ____

- **What are those things that make you forget time, lose track of time?**

____

____

____

____

____

____

____

- **When was the last time you lost track of time, because you were so involved** with doing the things you love to do?

____

____

____

____

____

____

- **Are there any topics that you can talk about for hours?**

- **Can you narrow down on one topic/one thing that you can talk about** for hours/do for hours without getting bored?

- **Is that also the one thing you would do if you had just 24 hours to live** (of course after spending time with your loved ones?)

___

___

___

___

___

___

___

- **What is something you would want to be forever remembered for,** even after you die?

___

___

___

___

___

___

- **Who would you choose to be if God grants you a wish, of living as your favorite person for a day?**

    ____

    ____

    ____

    ____

    ____

    ____

    ____

Can you find a common thread in all your answers?

You know where to reach out if you would like a 121 discussion on this: themerakiwoman

Find Your Essence

The *incident* I keep talking about is that one day out of thin air, I lost Sumedh, a whole human, a force of life, just gone.

And that made me add this dimension to it.

Who are you exactly, without the successful titles you hold? A soul, dressed as a human in flesh and blood. The purpose of your existence goes beyond finding your superpower. It is finding your essence. Meeting your authentic self, learning all the lessons you came here to learn, as a soul.

Why do only a few people make it big, despite them doing everything they can in their power? Because there are other things at play too.

- Your upbringing (what family you are born into, what values were you taught, what values you follow as you grow up)
- Your skill sets (tangible, intangible)
- Your destiny (past life karmas, lessons and how much access to have to free will depending on this life's karmas)

I have been a restless soul, chasing some distant goal all my life, without pausing to think, if that aligned with my essence, my home frequency or not.

End of the day, we are all just energies of different frequencies, and we all have a place in the scheme of things.

You may or may not conquer the world, but you certainly are the world for someone.

You may have made choices in the past that you wish you could take back; but forgive yourself because you chose what you felt was right at that time, with your sense of understanding back then. As long as your intentions are good, it is the learning that matters.

Find Your Essence comes from the perfume brand The Musk Wear, that I am about to launch. Musk means Kasturi, found in the navel of a particular type of deer. The deer keeps wandering trying to find the source of that fragrance, unaware that what he is looking on the outside is actually within.

It's time we become aware of what is inside, what is our essence, because when we start showing ourselves as exactly who we are, we start attracting what is meant for us, not just as a human, but as a soul, at a deeper level of existence.

Your superpower will come to you as an effect of finding your own essence.

Few things that will come handy in arriving there.

1. Showing up as YOU

In the book *The Mountain is You*, a powerful line resonates:

"When you start showing up as exactly who you are, you start radically changing your life."

But here's the question: how many of us truly show up as *exactly* who we are? And deeper still – how many of us even *know* who we are?

Most of our understanding of self comes from years of conditioning – what others expect us to be, the habits we pick up, or the roles we play in response to our surroundings. It's like scrolling through your social media feed. You like one fitness video, engage with a productivity post, and suddenly your feed is flooded with similar content. Who you are becomes a reflection of external influences, shaped by repetition.

But take a break – step away from the noise – and something shifts. When you return, the feed is different, and so is your perspective.

This mirrors real life:

- ***Who you are*** **is often how others perceive you – labels like "helpful," "mean," or "loving."**
- ***What you know about who you are*** **is your internal truth – your motivations, fears, and desires.**

Someone who comes across as mean may simply be protecting themselves from past hurt. A jovial person might be masking their pain. Someone who is helpful all the time may actually be struggling to say "no." – overcompensating for something or feeling like an imposter. That is the difference between *what you know* about who you are and who you are.

The deeper *knowing* comes from stepping back, reflecting, and doing the inner work.

And here's the key: showing up authentically requires courage. It's not about being perfect or having all the answers. It's about peeling back the layers and standing in your truth. You may not like what you find. But remember, light and dark are sides of the same coin. It's not good or bad, it is just light and dark, both together make an absolute truth. Don't reject yourself, don't reject your dark, embrace it the way you would embrace your light.

This is the first step to discovering your essence; because from this point onwards, it is not good or bad, it is only acceptance and channelizing.

Activity: How do people describe you? How will you describe yourself and why? Is it the same, is it different? Talk to yourself, write to yourself.

2. Fluidity over Fixation

Finding out who you are is not a destination but an ongoing journey – a process of discovering different parts of yourself, allowing them to evolve, and embracing the fluidity of change.

For years, I believed I was someone who would never get a tattoo. It became a part of my self-definition. But then, something shifted. I got one, then another, and now those tattoos are part of my story. The non-tattoo version of me was valid, and so is this version. Both are equally true, because growth doesn't invalidate the past; it builds on it.

The key to evolution lies in giving yourself permission to change – without judgment. True change feels good from the inside out, not just as a reaction to external triggers. When you allow yourself to explore who you are without fear of "right" or "wrong," you begin to discover the beauty of authentic growth.

Society often primes us to follow a predefined path: get an education, land a respectable job, get married, raise kids, and teach them to do the same. It's not "wrong," but it's just one version of "right" – one that has been deemed acceptable by collective belief.

I've come to see that there are no absolute rights or wrongs, only different truths. What's right for one person may not align with another's journey, and that's okay. As Dr. Siddharth Warrior, a neurologist and digital thought leader, wisely pointed out: spirituality is self-discovery. By its very nature, it can't have mass appeal. Subjecting self-discovery to societal validation dilutes its essence.

Your truth is yours alone. Mine is mine. They don't need to match to be valid. Coexisting with differing truths is the foundation of authentic living – and ultimately, branding.

Think of self-discovery like emotions. Feelings – anger, sadness, jealousy – are not inherently good or bad. They simply are. What matters is how you respond to them. Do you let them flow through you, or do you hold onto them, letting them shape your identity?

When you stay fluid, you avoid becoming fixated as "the angry young man" or "the anxious woman." Instead, you remain open to change, letting emotions move through you until only clarity remains. Fluidity is what allows you to adapt, evolve, and grow into the person – and brand – you're meant to be.

Activity: Any conflicting beliefs you have grown up with? Felt like *rights*, when others taught it as '*wrongs*'. How are you feeling right now about those beliefs? Write down about your fears, insecurities, motivators.

3. Happyholic or Workaholic?

Work can consume you when you actually love what you are doing. If you know what that means you are a happyholic, not a workaholic.

But a majority of people are clocking in hours just for the sake of it, because so often we equate the number of hours as work done or putting in the hard work, when it could really be donkey work.

All I am saying is I totally come from the same school of thought that hard work is irreplaceable and there will be times when you may have to work 18 hours a day; do it because it brings you joy because only then it means 18 happy hours in a day, not forced unhappy hours.

When choosing a career path, no pain is never the choice. You have to struggle to be a doctor or to be a writer, but make the struggle worth it.

Here's a video I saw on YouTube:

One day, in a class of 30 odd kids of grade 5, a teacher decides to play some interactive games. She distributes plain paper and a color pen to every student.

She then turns to the blackboard and writes this Q there – *'What do you want to be when you grow up?'*

She asks the students to write the answer to this Q and display the paper over their heads for her to see.

Some of them have traditional answers like Doctor, Engineer, Lawyer etc; some of them are unconventional answers like YouTuber, Gamer, Actor, Writer etc.

But there's one answer that leaves the teacher confused.

She goes up to the student and asks him with concern as to why he wrote what he wrote. Did he not understand the meaning of the question on the blackboard? She tries to explain to him the kind of answers that were expected by giving examples of other students and their answers.

The student looks at the teacher with innocent questioning eyes and replies, "Teacher, my mother is a doctor, my father is a lawyer, my elder brother is studying engineering and everyday at the dinner table they all crib and complain about how their lives are.

So many times, we don't even have dinner together. Makes me wonder if they are all sad. Are you also sad, teacher? All I want to do when I grow up is be happy, with whatever I do."

He continues earnestly, "I don't quite know what I will be growing up. One day I want to be a doctor but the very next day I feel like becoming a dancer. It's very confusing to me. But I am sure that I want to keep smiling and be happy – be it as a doctor or a dancer. And that's possible, right?"

The teacher learnt a lesson that day, smiled at the kid and said, "It's the best answer ever."

It all comes back to self-awareness. The more you connect with your authentic self, the more meaningful your pursuits become.

Your superpower isn't external. It's not in a cape or waiting for a radioactive spider to find you. It's inside you – buried under layers of societal conditioning, generational trauma, and self-limiting beliefs.

Uncovering it requires you to stop chasing and start listening to yourself. Because your authentic self doesn't just know your path – it *is* your path.

Apne aap ko ek mauka toh do....

Activity: What was it that you loved doing as a kid? Something that you were also ridiculously effortlessly good at. Maybe the answer to your essence, your superpower has its roots in your childhood happy memories.

4. Help yourself first.

I am going to write something straight-up from a book, that I keep going back to, that has kept me sane all along and that literally makes me a better person every time I read it.

It's a book titled, Big Magic by Elizabeth Gilbert, who is more popular for her novel Eat Pray Love, which got adapted into a Julia Roberts starring film.

The paragraph I am going to quote appeals to me more as a writer but it is relevant for anyone in the creative field. I deeply resonate with it more in my 30's than I could in my 20's.

And while 'creativity' is something that everyone can use irrespective of any field, this paragraph is particularly dedicated to those in the 'creative field.'

Here goes:

Oh, and there's another thing: You are not required to save the world with your creativity.

Your art not only doesn't have to be original, in other words; it also doesn't have to be *important.*

For example: Whenever anybody tells me they want to write a book in order to help other people, I always think, *Oh, please don't.*

Please don't try to help me.

I mean, it is very kind of you to want to help people, but please don't make it your sole creative motive. I would so much rather that you wrote a book in order to entertain yourself than to help me. Or if your subject matter is darker and more serious, I would prefer that you made your art in order to save yourself, or to relieve yourself of some great psychic burden, rather than to save or relieve us.

I once wrote a book in order to save myself. I wrote a travel memoir in order to make sense of my own journey and my own emotional confusion. All I was trying to do with that book was figure myself out. In the process though, I wrote a story that apparently helped a lot of other people figuring themselves out. If I'd sat down to write Eat Pray Love with the sole aim of helping others, I would've produced an entirely different book.

Consider this very book, for example, which you are right now holding in your hands. Big Magic is obviously a self-help guide, right? But with all the due respect and affection, I did not write this book for you; I wrote it for me. I wrote this book for my own pleasure, because I truly enjoy thinking about the subject of creativity. It's enjoyable and useful for me to meditate on this topic. If what I have written here ends up helping you, that's great, I will be glad. That would be a wonderful side effect. But at the end of the day, I do what I do because I like doing it.

It's okay if your work is fun for you, is what I'm saying. It's also okay if your work is healing for you, or fascinating for you or redemptive for you, or if it's maybe just a hobby that keeps you from going crazy. It's even okay if your work is totally frivolous. That's allowed. It's all allowed.

Your own reasons to create are reason enough. Merely by pursuing what you love, you may inadvertently end up helping us plenty.

Do whatever brings you to life, then. Follow your own fascinations, obsessions and compulsions. Trust them. Create whatever causes a revolution in your heart. The rest of it will take care of itself.

Activity: Do you recall doing anything like this? That you did just for YOU, you just played you, and it helped someone!

I am doing this right now. Helping myself with this book.

I was reeling with a lot of self-doubt when I started writing this book. And I did start off with 'wanting to help people' and somewhere on the path realized that this is more about helping my own self. I was also sitting on the book idea for quite some time because I asked myself "why would anyone pick this up and read, who am I really?"

Who am I, really, that people will pick this book? I haven't accomplished as much that will put me on pedestal for others to choose this book, just because I have written it.

To write a self-help book, don't you have to help yourself first? I mean, obviously, right? I should have it all figured out, if I claim to 'self-help' other people. But I don't have it all figured out.

I only have that much figured, right now, that I know, will lead to the next step of figuring out.

This realization, rather this sense of self-awareness that has come to me (I have paid quite a price for it, hasn't really come to me easy) gave me the courage to take this up at a state when I am still a work-in-progress project myself. But yes, progress is the important word here.

And Life has taught me quite recently that, *that* much is enough (most of the times); life reveals to you only how much you can handle. Sometimes, knowing too much at the wrong time can do more harm than help.

It might be hard to agree to this, but try and give this a thought.

'Trusting' how much you know 'in the moment' is more important than anything else; because no one has it all figured out.

You do you, me do me – let this be the new mantra for co-creation :)

5. Destiny or Free Will?

A million dollar question, isn't it? The answer is both. There are times when something pre-defined, predestined holds more power over you. And there are times when your freewill is the most powerful.

All our scriptures, every story in there, take any character, you will see everything is connected. Butterfly effect is a simple translation to everything being connected.

Where Abhimanyu was able to realise his destiny and purpose right from when he was in his mother's womb, and it happened for Shabari at a ripe old age.

We see young achievers, gifted musicians and we know it's something they have carried from somewhere beyond our understanding.

Since the whole premise of this book is two most life impacting decisions – love and career – we see people around us who seem to be doing everything right and still feeling stuck.

My only words to them are, keep at it, there will come a time when your destiny & freewill will make friends with each other and attracting from your home frequency will seem like a well thought well structured play, than some random jigsaw puzzle.

One day, everything will fall in place. You will find your essence and your superpower too. You will navigate yourself, well.

Activity: Feel free to take a moment to pause. Doddle, scribble or leave it blank.

Random thoughts:

My notes:

Scribbles and doodles…

My notes:

My notes:

www.ingramcontent.com/pod-product-compliance
Lightning Source LLC
LaVergne TN
LVHW091318150826
845673LV00006B/1693